HIGH MARSH ROAD

High Marsh Road

lines for a Diary, by DOUGLAS LOCHHEAD

GOOSE LANE

Published by Goose Lane Editions with the assistance of the Canada Council and
the New Brunswick Department of Municipalities, Culture and Housing, 1996.
Originally published by Anson-Cartwright Editions, 1980.

ACKNOWLEDGEMENTS: *Descant, Matrix*, The Canada Council.

Original edition designed by C. Freeman Keith and printed by Stinehour Press.
Cover photograph by Thaddeus Holownia.
Printed in Canada by Tribune Printing.
  10 9 8 7 6 5 4 3 2

Canadian Cataloguing in Publication Data
  Lochhead, Douglas, 1922-
    High marsh road
    Poems.
    ISBN 0-86492-192-6

  I. Title.
  PS8523.o33H44 1996   C811'.54   C96-950033-5
  PR9199.3.L63H44 1996

Goose Lane Editions
469 King Street
Fredericton, New Brunswick
CANADA E3B 1E5

The High Marsh Road crosses the Tantramar Marshes from near Middle and Upper Sackville to the Aulac Ridge. It is a dirt road and takes the days and nights as they come. In September the farm trucks raise dust which the winds quickly carry with them over the wide expanse of marsh grasses. By December the ruts have hardened and there is ice and snow. The Road is very much a part of the Marsh.

To live near the Tantramar is to be conscious of its brooding, changing and always beautiful presence. On the High Marsh Road one's thoughts stay with minute details of mouse tracks or harrier or they move with the past, with people, all quite personal.

One goes to the Marsh often. It envelops. One emerges with brief accounts, often epigrammatic statements, with lines for a diary. At least this is one man's experience with Tantramar and the High Marsh Road.

DL
Sackville
New Brunswick
1980

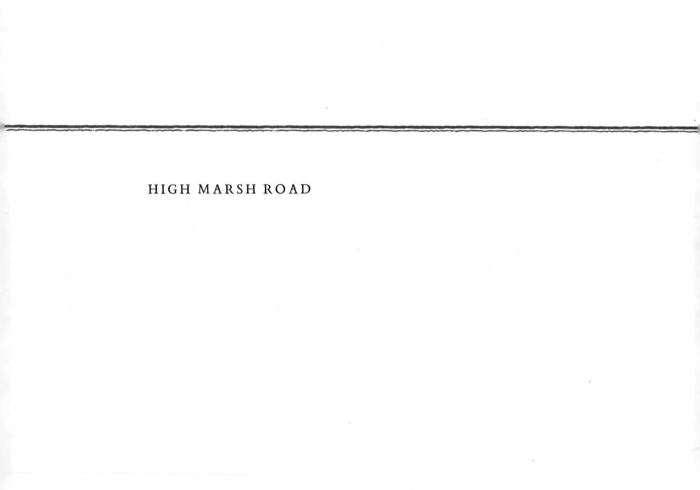

HIGH MARSH ROAD

Colville's crow mounts higher higher.
the silver spoon is fast in the beak.
what behind eye prompts bird to seize
such objects and hide them away?

SEPTEMBER 2

---

here, right where my foot takes weight,
what Acadian sweated and froze in the
ever-wind to make these dykes? there *is*
a sense of history here and all across
this marsh

SEPTEMBER 3

the river, the Tantramar, is narrow, deep,
tidal. to fall in is not to be found.
so close to all that power. cleansing

the poet waits. the heart opens.
he trips over the plank and drowns in it.
the red sea of his singing

SEPTEMBER 5

I begin myself foot before foot
along the red road. whitethroats
find seed. snow buntings wait for
about a month. I find only the
echoes hung up on a stinging wind.
to believe in a name would be a beginning
having given up renewals at least for a
while. it is nothing at all to crush
part of oneself let alone another

SEPTEMBER 6

you will wait. at least I hope that
will be the way of it. wait while I
tend the sleeping faces in the
marsh and crawl out wearing
a face you will recognize. it
will not be easy for you

Spartina the name of grasses.
sea-lavender a bloom of it
today

SEPTEMBER 8

---

simplify, simplify. turning
inwards to make the decision
could mean we shall see the
day out

the heart renews. this is
a large part of the miracle.
I am on the hunt for love,
this being that kind of day

SEPTEMBER 10

you grin, a private one. I
know I have done something
right. an instant is enough
for most things

SEPTEMBER 11

today it will keep on raining.
weather is in all our calculations.
the panic field looks deserted
but even without binoculars I
detect movement. someone else
is breathing out there

why bury yourself in this place you
ask. yes I hear you. what makes
me stammer a bit is the difficulty
I have in finding just the few right
words to tell you there will be no
funeral

you come again from such distances
to remind me that something has happened.
it is your silence which comes

dear x.

   it is of course the silence to which
I have referred elsewhere. this is the
killing or loving thing between two. here
is the killing. and there is nothing to be
done about it, because, admit it, at least
to yourself, you and I are too timid, really
too much afraid to do *something* (at least
something would be better). so now the
non-letters I continue to not receive breathe
a heavy breath and it makes this place leap
up and fall back . . . . how do you set characters

now, the metal ones in the stick or do some
of the glancing moves remind you of me and
spoil it because it is no escape, is it?
perhaps there will be something tomorrow . . . .
I doubt it wise one

the road banks abruptly at this place.
red earth pushed back by unnatural
machines. the intrusion is noticeable
and will remain on the marsh-face as
cancer

SEPTEMBER 16

---

you will get on with it. the High Marsh
Road has taken a beating from every truck
on Friday rum-with-beer night in Sackville.
it can take mine

shrugging off yesterday. the past is
a vast pit. it is always from darkness
that we work and sometimes there is
light. when it lasts it is called joy.
some have trouble recognizing it. others
fail pitifully not knowing it exists

the main theme in our poetry
is terror or some call it fear.
to be told this the first reaction
is to laugh. so is the second

there are too many faces I seem
to recognize in the parade of
clouds today

---

this new space. this new sky.
I find myself with my eyes.
there is no need to stand up in it

the short hair and the hands on
hips. hard wrists and forearms
out of three-quarter length shirt
sleeves. I want to be tough again.
it will do everyone good

the horse limps out of the covered
bridge. a girl leads it. she is
teaching it to go into darkness. into
new noises, silences. into darkness.
yes

this is the place. the marsh. to
keep beginning from such horizons.
it is the fact, the main one, the
constant looking out. goldfinches
finding seeds. day after day

there is no doubt that you are a
character. the town marsh-boy.
walks anywhere. what is in the
bag? any time you can see him.
he is there. will I know this
person?

SEPTEMBER 25

---

the road is slightly wet from the
night's near frost. cobwebs become
silver sirens between grasses and twigs.
it is zero in September. movement
everywhere

the barns on the marsh. small
blocks fallen as toys. the
mind investigates from this distance
telling me that they are weathered,
hung with hay, places for owls

why not turn just ahead beyond
the covered bridge? there is a
good view of the river. several
turns. heron and greater yellow
legs are often in there

over the hill is Northumberland Strait.
long lines. its tide covers the flats,
the sand places for snail, mussel, clam.
I saw a dowitcher. nine ruddy turnstones.
now I see their name. that is what the autumn
coloured wonders were doing. turning the flat
red sandstones over. searching the high-tide
weeds

SEPTEMBER 29

there is song in these seasons. the
Tintemarre. ghost birds over the
centuries. voices in the tape of
wind. caught. to come back in their
times. Tintemarre

who ever sees the fire at its brightest?

OCTOBER 1

night. damp. the black cougar was sighted.
several miles from here into the marsh
where there are tamarack and spruce.
the forests of the night cougar

this morning cold. what awakened
me to it were the sounds of
the rum-dipped duck hunters
firing in broken bursts

---

the clouds are beyond fetching, and
beyond the blind hunters. beyond
all the mouths whose lips smell of
corruption. it is their mindless
conspiracy to kill. to kill with
as much as a glare, the innocents,
the good ones. this is what
gets me down

the matching petals. how alike;
as I come closer your breasts
are almost motionless but the
shadows, textures and tones make
differences

OCTOBER 5

---

the time to rest the eyes and fling
them far like stars. they fall on
the marsh and become mushrooms
for other people to pick up

light glances on the puddles along
the High Marsh Road. October about
this time of the month is for
geese and they continue to fly high,
very high. I have seen none touch
down this autumn

OCTOBER 7

---

it is the morning to see a Rousseau
sun. the wide marsh takes the
long rays as they push up
details of grasses, wild birds
(wilder somehow in this place because
it is so much theirs). so many things
emerge with the orange light of it

the real round of the saying never forms,
but the poet is constantly working, moulding
it closer and closer to the truth

the total glimpse of it as Roberts
took to Tantramar. using his telescope
his eye revisited. now I search the
same dykes for details of shore-birds.
the weirs hold straggler ducks. it is
good to have such footsteps

OCTOBER 10

at once it was good. our meeting
solitary in a hospitality room full
of noise. yes it was very good.
the walking in utter quiet brings
it all back. good

dear x.

   you have made notes to put into a letter.
this you told me. you are afraid that
whatever you say will give the wrong
emphasis. will encourage me. lead me on.
I am my age and I listen to all of this.
it *does* make sense. you want to avoid
hurting me who now hide behind three-foot
walls. yes, once I did get the wrong
idea and I let it take off. leading to
nothing. I don't mind. nothing hurts
anymore. this you must tell yourself.
please write

OCTOBER 12

the colours take over. long
banners of green, white and hard blue
stream into abstractions. in the
fog the marsh vanishes

---

the number of times I have said yes.
non, non et non. my mouth is
already formed

I give way. crawl inside
myself. the thought of such
ruling bastards troubles my
innocence. this must stop.
remember your age

another day. anguished muscles
of cloud and wind drive me to
ground. I lie in an empty field.
only dreams are warm

---

the poet. yes. but taken apart who
is this lurcher, lecher, big bear talker,
bull in a word-shop? when the mirror says
so much, I hesitate to look at the remains
of the others. fellow poets rot with me

the continual measuring. wishing for
otherwise. the great game of 'if'. no,
it could not be me but Harry. the hands
of the world close on all of us into
fists and we are nut shells

these are my fifties. never have I
been so aware. so clear about it.
every day (and night) new disguises.
over the familiar (unknown?) face grows
a strange mask. the lines harden.
deepen. a crazy grid in so many directions

---

this is my place. it is for me to tell
you. coming from inside. the mind
is not enough. I must take all
signals. events. the accident
at any moment can wreck worlds.
yours and mine

the wild frenzy for life. the streaming
constellations make statements I fail
to hear night after night. the blind and
the deaf and the fight going on in the
crush of silence

I move with the harrier. the mole
is my nestling lover. roots I trace
and cover myself with the green
and brown rot. what face to see,
to write down? each feature a
mockery. a saint unfolds. there
is a wild marriage of detail. who
will arrange it? it is my doing

the same wind. without such great measures.
how do I bring such details for all to see.
in this basket of your skirt? underneath
the details continue. what brought you five
thousand miles for this? why questions?

your visit was all planned.
my own disney land. to show
you marsh. find a harrier. buy
lobster. take wine. these
would be our observances. rituals
before love. a dirty dragging
hope it all was too. where the
hell did you go?

---

sea time. out there is Chignecto. in from
it the tidal grasses are wind-churned on
Tantramar. skitters of shorebirds

OCTOBER 25

first frost to kill. there is not
much left on the marsh. a hint of
ice in ruts. the mists will not
burn off until ten. then the cold
feel of it will be gone

---

you will give me a shotgun.
the ammunition I already have.
you will go along that side.
I will cover this. I will
throw ammo and all into the river.
this is my plan

the fields are raw. goldfinches
are after seeds. they keep the
place alive. who is there with me
to watch their bouncy-flight?
they are busy until dark

thin snow lying almost until noon
then lapsing into green. the first
fall came in the night. I did
not see it but I did hear the
geese high and honking. telling,
telling

OCTOBER 29

I arrived late. over there three ducks
in worried flight. the stars dominate.
some are heavy with light. a comfort
of dark. the strange embrace of it

a golden plover, then another.
solitaries but together. their
sudden drama. at least as I see
it. will they get past the hunters?
they only understand buckshot.
stalk them in their pickup trucks
and shave them with a shot

yes, but something will turn up.
something will come of it all. the
road will remain. echoes of all
this picked up. Charles G. D.
Roberts, pince-nez and tails, flies
like an angel by Stanley Spencer over
this place

the red clay gone brown under
rotting hay fits the black clouds
of my bitter wonder

love is like the hay, is cut down
and what I have seen of it lies
unraked, souring all it touches.
at that the cut was unexpected.
who is to tell me how long this
will last? I want to know

---

frost on the marsh makes white
fossils of the past month's growth.
the sting of cold is now in the bones
of it

NOVEMBER 4

---

day upon day upon the
bumping agony of each one.
a free fall waits for each
one of us

how does the wind catch your hair and
leave it that way? even in storm
warnings you continue to glisten

the black cougar is there this night. with
such stars, cold, and no moon, it must
move out to kill. all this within a
few miles. how do *we* come to grips?

NOVEMBER 7

---

the son-of-a-bitch of a critic never
read the book and then sneered down
his columbian nose at what was not in it.
this goes on in this country. all of
the time

the wind cleanses. grey overhang
turns boiling with cloud-roll to
blue. this daily turnaround never
misses

---

he gave me a worry stone.
John was always a giver. it
was a ceremony. your death now,
almost a year back was that way.
your occasion. how crafty you were.
and wise

again wind heavy against the
marsh. the clouds rip apart
with noise. a harrier stoops
and goes again

dear x.
   you have not put your notes together. they
have not arrived in the form of a letter.
silences begin to harden, deepen and my curses
begin to threaten my whistling. in the long
run this is good. more practice for more pain

dear x.
   if there is no letter tomorrow I
will give up on you. there is no
other way. now that we have talked so
little time ago I know your silence
could be a self-inflicted wound

NOVEMBER 13

---

dear x.
    I translate this way. it is the only
way I know. why should I change after
all this? leave or take but give me
the facts. from your own hand please

NOVEMBER 14

---

the High Marsh Road is frozen hard.
it is mid–November. yet for almost
a week there has been straight sun
and straight blue. there is an edge
to the staying cold

NOVEMBER 15

---

down a tube of air the harrier goes.
today he is distant, absorbed

---

what is told by one of the corners
of Christopher Pratt's windows? we
can never go very deep. yet the window
is everywhere

someone said sorrow springs from
the earth. curse it. remorse hangs
on every November tree. head for the
marsh my friend

a hymn sung in a bar. why not?
the blonde woman is all music.
all woman. dare. dare

your hair moves, flares about your
head and it is the motion of the
stars. Was it Rodin who said that?

---

snow blown over the marsh. the
cold white undoes the flames only
a little. each has its own set of
rules. part of the order

NOVEMBER 21

---

underneath the heaped hay is snow-covered.
the slow turning and mingling and
twisting of life goes on

I realize it has been a life of
corners for me. once or twice have
I realized this. rare as joy. the
first step, you guessed it, simplify

---

reading the ciphers across the barren.
the codifier, the sweeping calligraphy
of the Tantramar wind. white plates for
printing a profile that is so close, so
difficult to read

the snow builds high tonight.
out there is wind. wind lives
a constant on the Tantramar. this
night is the coldest yet. what does
the cougar do on such nights but peer
and starve

NOVEMBER 25

---

you will understand better if you test
the day. take people as they are. the
long suffering is in all of us. I am just
about, no, I am ready, to say: well so-what
sun, moon, stars! Yahoo is my name

this road is a high wire. inch by inch.
I am still upright. the bar of balance
makes it a near thing when the wind blows.
inch by bloody inch

NOVEMBER 27

it is the dead who sing. who is
to match their great chorus? I
bend to them in this graveyard at
Jolicure. only the flag on my
friend's plot waves. there is the
murmur of his voice. word after
word. there is no forgetting John.
whatever tack I take

road. road. the ruts firm up.
run along the frozen rails. the
tracks unloose the mind. such
details. mere ones are eyes, ears,
touchies. the works

to place it. after saying it. let
laughter sit on the right throne.
thunder-mug of words. the blown
ecstasy. today new planks on an
old barn. broken ice. still shell.
the ancient hinges breed a swing door.
night music

I was out in it all day. sudden
November hard. laughed, laughed.
waving wild arms. flew above
birds in a spindle-legged crazy
joy

lying spread out and with my eye
at such an angle, you are the contour
of this place. your thighs, your hairy
rise, the breasts modelled to you. yes,
you are it. you are this place

the poem unleashes a series of locks,
traps and trip-wires

reminders of age, unexpected, but
whittling away at us. in the long
run it will be best. to be honed
this way for death

DECEMBER 4

---

an Arctic owl on a power pole.
here to stay two months going through
his actions. the mouse. the mole

poet as hunter. what a picture.
bending over the trap, slipping
a cartridge in, finally the
mouth takes the barrel
and trigger finds the quarry

DECEMBER 6

---

now to the leaping fields where
several barns as boxes stand
empty. now to the chase
around and through. all the
angles, lights and darks
of dreams

DECEMBER 7

---

in all this I try to look head on.
who in all this place will look
back? return the first serve? in
the country you find it harder
to hear the answer, to admit what
burns holes inside

the echoes keep coming. they are
stubborn. it is a question of learning
how to use them

---

these words are messages for those
who would receive them. gone is
time for argument

head on. at least that. but you
shrivel like the hairy mole. what
am I doing? now is time to ask
again

every day there is more defiance.
the voice. the sudden wild laugh.
this is a new part of me worth
watching

DECEMBER 12

give out for me because your
help is all I want. the great
northern enclosures, the chains
of stars are strangely silent
when there should be joy

it is here. I take it.
the hard road, frozen, wind-whipped.
all this I must *see*. a
belly-fool of facts. then it is up
to me to apply

now take Vermeer. with all this
light this day he would have gone
berserk. simple as that. berserk
with love. brushes idle

---

all day it has been the cleaning
up of things. the mind with its last
flags, old trophies. I want to
live the way of bright banners. to
the marsh. let me out

DECEMBER 16

---

the whole day shaken. a convulsion
of sudden wind spinning the few
birds. dark clouds add all the elements
of seizures and grip the marsh. it is flat.
harsh itself. it lies low waiting the
fit out

DECEMBER 17

---

almost the end of the year. the footsteps
along the Marsh Road are frozen into
grey-blue craters. now it is beginning
to blow rain. over everything is the grey
close. after the return I was soaked but
alive

DECEMBER 18

is there anything to report? the way
of weather, harriers, the marsh, this
place of road, all are outside. we are
included just as that snowy owl there.
the mind envelops. on the surface
everything moves to its
own level. now I see

the ski tracks on the marsh snow.
someone else before me. breaking
them first. leaning where the wind is.
it is good to follow these unknown
marks. they are fresh, immediate,
just done. the breaker out of sight

dear x.
   we were all over without a start.
the tease went deep into my pleasure—
dome of roaring fancies. all gone
without appearing. I feel good.
clean. the purity of such a birth.
I was on the high marsh all day.
because of you. and saw nothing

dear x.
    now you have a child. this is
good news. it must be said another
way. you really did not tell me.
you had put on weight. there it
was. everyone has his madonna.
in some strange way you are mine.
the image burns. there is no pain
in it. the fire is yours. in the
child. in those green and grey eyes

DECEMBER 22

go grip something. the lack of
anything but this turf. rock-hard.
the shield in Sackville. winter
moves

the loins collapse. the cold you
left has seized me, the marsh,
the place. what was the point?
coming closer. tongue. that
would have shoved the knife home
sooner

ice over all. no moon.
the cold cracks underneath.
ice-noise. what goings-on.
flat. blue-black night.
the crack of it

DECEMBER 25

today it is Christmas. birth and
the celebration. the crazy busyness.
we should all fast and spend time on
our knees

DECEMBER 26

---

the year winds down in a gossip of
Christmas. let the babe alone.
put out one candle. walk in the
woods where the branches break with
cold. it is to come

the snow turns in the wind.
into a shell's whorl. what
breaks here to make it so?
the immensity of small. in
all this is refuge

the form. your form. the one I
saw earlier is still with me. my
cheek is on the snow's face. I
grovel into your heap of it. what
strange warmth. the lips carry it.
mole again. deeper. the strangled.
unexpected. here. the marsh. the
closing bed. you remember

---

the patterns of my boots were first
signs. looking back the sober track
fits. this marsh going to great flares
of line. in all directions. the lines
are part of the barns. now there is noise.
a thin thrashing, in the dry hay. what
stirs? the year shakes loose for one last
time. this day. and tomorrow

of course this is celebration. what
stars I do not see I celebrate.
give joys to burnt out stars.
I am one of them. where is light?
are there new fables? I hope so.
find some music. I want
to dance

you come out of a bank of breakers.
sea-swells of night-beginning cloud.
marshalling of storms. the music
heaves. the conductor is Charlie
Chaplin. laughter adds to the
noise of bells, breakers and buoys

Douglas Lochhead was born in Guelph, Ontario, and grew up in Fredericton and Ottawa. After serving as an infantry officer in the Canadian Army during World War II and working as an advertising copywriter, Lochhead worked as a librarian and taught English at universities in the United States, Canada, and Scotland, including Cornell, Dalhousie, York, Toronto, Edinburgh and Mount Allison. From 1963 to 1975, he was Librarian and a Senior Fellow at Massey College at the University of Toronto. In 1975, he became the Davidson Professor of Canadian Studies at Mount Allison University and, in 1987, the university's first Writer-in-Residence. He is now Professor Emeritus of Canadian Studies, Mount Allison University; Senior Fellow and Founding Librarian of Massey College, University of Toronto; and a Fellow of the Royal Society of Canada.